PHOTOGRAPHY BASICS

by
Vick Owens-Knudsen

Introduction by
Dennis Simonetti

Photographs by the
**Students of
Glen Rock Junior and Senior High School**

Diagrams and Drawings by
Mike Petronella

Created and Produced by
Arvid Knudsen

16255

Prentice-Hall, Inc.
Englewood Cliffs, New Jersey

DEDICATION

To my many talented and devoted photography
students, and to our many happy hours in the
darkroom, the shared learning, the joy of producing good prints, and the excitement of success
with new techniques—all of which have played a
part in making this book a reality.

Acknowledgements

My special thanks to the Glen Rock, New
Jersey, Board of Education, Dr. Betty Ostroff-
Carpenter, Superintendent of Schools, and to
Mr. Ed Turco, Principal of Glen Rock Jr./Sr.
High School for their strong support, encourage-
ment and vision given the photography program
for our young people.

My deepest gratitude to Joel Shumer and Craig
Vargabedian, both fine photographers in their
own right, for their valuable suggestions and interest in *Photography Basics*.

Editor's Note: Our thanks to the Eastman Kodak Company,
Minolta Corporation and Nikon, Inc. for their help with
product materials and camera information.

Text Copyright © 1983 by Vick Owens-Knudsen
and Arvid Knudsen

Illustrations and Photographs © 1983 by Arvid Knudsen

Book Design by Arvid Knudsen

Printed in the United States of America.   -J

Prentice-Hall International, Inc., London
Prentice-Hall of Australia, Pty. Ltd., Sydney
Prentice-Hall Canada, Inc., Toronto
Prentice-Hall of India Private Ltd., New Delhi
Prentice-Hall of Japan, Inc., Tokyo
Prentice-Hall of Southeast Asia Pte. Ltd., Singapore
Whitehall Books Limited, Wellington, New Zealand
Editora Prentice-Hall Do Brasil LTDA., Rio de Janeiro

10 9 8 7 6 5 4 3   1

Library of Congress Cataloging in Publication Data

Owens-Knudsen, Vick.
  Photography basics.

  (Technology basics books)
  Includes index.
  Summary: An introduction to basic techniques of
photography and various types of cameras and
their uses. Includes a glossary of terms.
  1. Photography--Juvenile literature. [I. Photography]
I. Knudsen, Arvid. II. Title. III. Series.
TR149.093 1983   770   83-9775
ISBN 013-664995-5

CONTENTS

Upper left, Megan Fuller. *Upper right,* Sue Zavari.
Lower left, Jordi Visser. *Lower right,* Hal Knapp

Introduction

Back in the middle thirties, while I was a student in high school, I was witness to a miracle. The occasion was the emergence of a photographic image under an eerie colored red light set up in a temporarily darkened room by one of the teachers who was helping us students prepare the photographic material for our yearbook. I was determined from this moment on to become a miracle worker myself and I set out to acquire the needed technical skills to accomplish my goal. Somewhere along the road through time, I realized that, for me at least, the real miracle was the ability to record and preserve forever those little moments from the past, flavored with my own particular "mind's eye vision," which were important to me. In short, photography became the means of forming my own memory bank to refer back to when time had dulled my real memory of those occasions.

This enlightenment made me also more fully aware of the other myriads of uses of photography in every field of life from photojournalism to medicine and many others.

This book, prepared by Vick Owens-Knudsen, an extremely sensitive person whose feelings on photography (and life) parallel my own, will aid the young student of today in acquiring the basic technical skills to become the "miracle workers" of tomorrow.

For all of us whose lives will be enriched by Ms. Owens-Knudsen's efforts I say "thank you, Vick."

Dennis Simonetti
Photographer and Teacher
PARSONS SCHOOL OF DESIGN
New School of Social Research

Joseph Niepce

Louis Jacques Daguerre

1 FLASHBACK: A Brief History

"It's a miracle!" said Sir John Herschel, the noted English chemist/astronomer, speaking about photography in 1839.

It is a miracle—a magic show, to be able to just point your camera, press the button, and have your picture—in a minute if you wish!

Originally, way back some 400 years ago, the camera was a darkened room with a tiny hole in one wall. It was called *camera obscura* in Italian. While standing inside the pitch-dark room, you could see what was in front of the pinhole on the opposite wall. The projected image was upside down. In the seventeenth to nineteenth centuries, the room finally became a portable box, still called camera obscura, fitted with a lens that could focus the image, adjust the light, and with an angled mirror turn the image right side up. The image was projected onto a translucent screen, where an artist could trace a selected scene. The 35mm single-lens reflex camera used today is based on the same design.

Although camera obscuras were long in use as copying machines, it was not until 1839 that a Frenchman named Louis Jacques Daguerre, using the research of Joseph and Isidore Niepce, applied chemical substances to a metal plate and by exposing the plate in the camera to light was able to imprint an image that would last. This was the first known practical photograph.

7

About the same time, William Henry Fox Talbott, an Englishman, invented a photo process called calotype that used a paper negative.

Nearly a century later his negative/positive process and his idea of using a lens that could intensify and concentrate light onto film were improved upon and became the ones most used in photography. Sir John Herschel shared many of his experiments for improving negatives and especially for "fixing" prints with Talbott.

The world accepted the metal "Daguerreotypes," and photography became the rage. In every city people wanted to prepare their own metal plates to catch the magic pictures. Optical and chemical supply houses were beseiged for lenses and chemicals. Balconies suddenly had wooden boxes pointed at the streets below, as amateur photographers waited for the right moment to remove the cork that covered the lens. To record an image could take anywhere from minutes to hours. As lenses improved and the boxes became smaller, photographers traveled to distant lands to photograph places of historic importance and natural wonders. Many artists and sculptors began to devote themselves seriously to photography and produced outstanding work.

The magic boxes were also pointed skyward to catch images of the moon and the constellations. People took their cameras up in balloons to capture a new view of the earth: an aerial perspective. There was a frenzy of picture taking. By 1880 cameras in Europe and America were made so small—because of improved lens design—that they were able to be hidden in walking sticks or concealed in clothing: neckties, handbags, and hats were popular places. Some 15,000 of these miniature vest-type "detective" cameras were sold within three years. They captured the public's imagination as novelties and produced the first unposed "candid" snapshots.

By 1890, George Eastman of the United States produced the "Brownie"—the most famous camera in history. It took good 2¼″ × 2¼″ pictures on cartridge-roll film, and it cost about a dollar. While the mass market played with the Brownie, the first twin-lens camera with two connecting lenses that focused simultaneously was designed and produced. This was followed by the first reflex camera.

The camera has grown in the refinement of its mechanics and the development of its lenses and has shrunk in size and weight to the convenience and delight of today's photographers.

Many courageous and skilled photographers have recorded important historic events with these types of cameras. There is a long list of perceptive and inventive masters, men and women whose work you will come to know as you become more involved with photography.

The early "Brownie" camera, the most popular camera in history.

Today's photography pioneers are already photographing the planets, searching into life's most minute matter, and learning about the deepest seas and the life they contain.

Probing the universe are the keyhole satellites nicknamed "spies of skies," for they can photograph details as small as the letters and numbers on a car's license plate from an altitude of 150 miles! By important advances in extending the focal length of telescopic lenses and replacing film with very sensitive electronic sensing devices, the impossible has become a reality. There are even optics that can correct distortions caused by the earth's atmosphere to give more accurate and precise photographs.

Electron micrography, at the other extreme, can produce photographs of an object that is magnified about a million times. This is done by recording signals, processed and amplified in various ways, to form an image on a cathode ray tube similar to the one in your TV set. The tube is hidden behind a built-in camera—a 35mm or 4″ × 5″ camera containing film such as Ilford's FP4 or Kodak's Plus-X or even Polaroid sheet film for instant pictures. The electronic microscopes can produce two- and three-dimensional photos. These fantastic instruments have uncovered a new world where giant viruses inhabit a surreal landscape that is a part of us, and where the common bug can appear as gigantic as the great dinosaurs that once roamed the earth.

There is no limit in sight, as photography probes the deepest mysteries of life and opens up new careers in all the endeavors of mankind—from probing the secrets of our bodies to probing the secrets of our earth and the universe.

BASIC PARTS
OF THE CAMERA

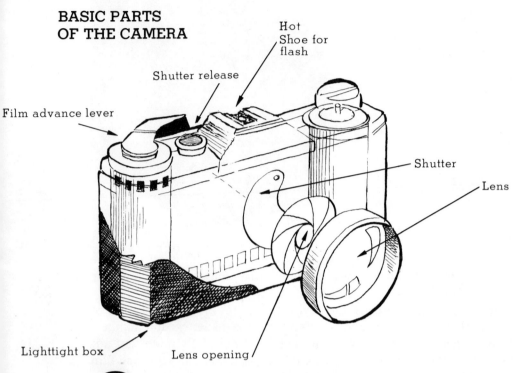

Hot
Shoe for
flash

Shutter release

Film advance lever

Shutter

Lens

Lighttight box

Lens opening

2 The Camera

The art of photography starts with the camera. Today's camera comes in unlimited sizes, varieties, and capabilities. What kind you begin with depends on your circumstances, your needs, and your purposes.

Cameras are light-tight boxes that have a light-gathering lens with adjusting control on one end and a place for film and a shutter on the other end. Included in the box are a means for advancing the film, a viewfinder to help frame your subject, a shutter release, a flash synchronizer, and countless other devices that provide convenience and control.

Some cameras have "aim and shoot" features that automatically focus your subject and set the exposure. These types are fine for average picture taking, where you allow the camera to make decisions for you and where you get the photograph without concern about apertures and shutter speeds. They are a great advantage for candid shots and recording events and places as a part of one's history.

The following is a breakdown of the cameras most commonly used today.

The Compact 35mm Camera

Basic features:

a. Uses 35mm roll film with 20 or 36 exposures.
b. Black-and-white or color prints enlarge to 5″ × 7″, 8″ × 10″, or 11″ × 14″ sizes; also makes color slides.
c. Automatic exposure.
d. Flash capability.
e. Lightweight: less than a pound.
f. Small size.

Other possible features: auto-focus, auto-wind and -rewind, auto-load, self-timer, built-in flash, and warning beeps and flashing lights to prevent errors.

The compact 35mm camera is a lightweight pocket-sized camera that is easy to use and carry. It is good for taking photos of your family and friends in normal activities under normal lighting conditions. This camera is moderately priced and is a good beginner's camera.

The Single-Lens Reflex Camera

Basic features:

a. Uses 35mm roll film with 20 or 36 exposures.
b. Black-and-white or color prints enlarge to 5″ × 7″, 8″ × 10″, or 11″ × 14″; also makes color slides.
c. Through-the-lens viewing.
d. Automatic and/or manual exposure control.
e. Self-timer for self-portraits.
f. Takes interchangeable lenses.

g. Flash capability includes flash shoe and flash outlet terminal.
h. Weighs under 1½ pounds.
i. Larger in size than the compact camera.

Other possible features: programmed exposure (totally automatic), interchangeable backs, and motorized attachment for (rapid) sequential shooting.

One of the most popular cameras in use today, the 35mm SLR camera can take many types of lenses, including zoom lenses; bellows (for close-up work) and motor drive (for advancing film). These plus other possible attachments make more creative shooting possible.

The SLR is an ideal camera to grow with.

The Disc Camera

Basic features:

a. Uses film disc with 15 exposures.
b. Easy loading.
c. Shoots only color film; makes 5″ × 7″ enlargements.
d. Automatic exposure.
e. Automatic film advance.
f. Automatically sets off built-in flash.
g. Capable of sequential shooting: three frames per second.
h. Shutter speeds can freeze moderate action: 1/200 of a second without flash and 1/100 of a second with flash.
i. Weighs less than one pound.

Kodak's disc camera features wafer-thin film discs. It is possibly the easiest camera to handle, but shoots only color. This is an ideal camera for family usage.

11

The Instant Camera

Basic features:

a. Uses film packs containing 10 exposures.
b. Easy loading.
c. Produces only color prints: $3\frac{1}{8}$" square. Copy prints can be made from wallet size to various enlargements; slides also can be made from original prints.
d. Prints are complete and ready for viewing within minutes.
e. Takes flash bar or flash attachment when flash is not built in.
f. Weighs less than one pound.

Other possible features: *provision for moderate close-ups; built-in flash.*

   The easy-to-use instant camera produces color prints that are fairly expensive. The camera is fun to use: just press the button and out comes the print.

Other Cameras:

110 Pocket Camera

Basic features:

a. Uses film cartridge.
b. Lens is either fixed-focus or uses focus symbols.
c. Bright line frame in viewfinder helps compose pictures.
d. Batteries power exposure metering and the electronic flash system.
e. Takes flash bar if without built-in flash.
f. Lightweight and fits in pocket.

The 110 pocket camera produces black-and-white (12 exposures) and color prints (12 and 24 exposures) that can be enlarged from $3\frac{1}{4}$" × $4\frac{1}{4}$" to 5" × 7" size. Color slides come in a 20-exposure cartridge. This camera is slowly being replaced by the 35mm compact and disc cameras.

The 126 Simple Camera

Basic features:

a. Uses film cartridge.
b. Produces square black-and-white and color prints (12 or 24 exposures) and color slides (20 exposures).
c. Variable lens openings.
d. Flash capability.
e. Lightweight.

   The 126 simple camera produces sharper prints than the 110 pocket camera because of its larger negative. Prints can be enlarged from 3" × 3" to 5" × 5" and 8" × 8". The camera will be replaced by the more advanced electronic cameras.

The Roll Film Camera

Basic features:

a. Uses 120- or 220- roll film (12 or 24 exposures).
b. Produces color or black-and-white prints or slides ($2\frac{1}{4}$" square).

c. Light meter required to guide exposure.
d. Viewing and focusing on a ground glass; image is reversed left to right.
e. Waist-level or eye-level viewing possible.
f. Interchangeable lenses and accessories.
g. Heavy in weight.
h. Bulky in size.

The larger negative and resulting sharpness of prints have encouraged photographers to continue using their heavy roll film cameras. The less bulky SLR (single lens reflex) 2¼" × 2¼" camera has largely replaced the roll film camera.

The View Camera
Basic features:
a. Uses 4" × 5" or 8" × 10" sheet film, depending on camera size.
b. Produces large negatives for sharp high-quality prints in color, black-and-white, or on instant film.
c. Viewing is on ground glass and requires an opaque viewing cloth. The image is seen upside down.
d. Requires separate light meter for exposure guide.

e. Contains bellows that tilt and swing to correct and distort images.
f. Capable of close-ups.
g. Made of wood.
h. Heavy.
i. Bulky.

The view camera is a professional camera. It is generally used on a tripod. Photo studios use view cameras for advertising photography and for portraits. In the field the camera is ideal for subjects requiring great detail and tonal range.

Ways to Hold Your Camera Steady

1. Make a tripod of your body by standing with legs comfortably apart, knees flexed, one foot slightly in front of the other and weight centered.
2. Make a shelf of your left hand and place the camera on it so that your thumb and index finger are able to curl around the lens barrel and turn the focusing ring.
3. Wind the shutter with the thumb of your right hand and release the shutter with the index finger.

4. *Press the camera against your forehead and hold your elbows close to your body.*
5. *Squeeze the shutter release button two thirds of the way down before actually taking the shot.*
6. *Brace yourself against a wall or post for support when using slow shutter speeds such as 1/30 or slower.*
7. *At shutter speeds slower than 1/30 use the self-timer to release the shutter automatically or use a tripod.*

Focusing

Cameras generally have at least one of three basic types of focusing aids: the split-image rangefinder circle, the microprism circle, and/or a ground-glass viewing screen.

Looking through the viewfinder (if your camera has the rangefinder circle), you will see a small centered circle divided into two halves. Select a post or any straight vertical edge. The edge will appear split or broken in the circle if your lens is not focused. Turn the focusing ring on the lens barrel until the split halves line up. Your object is now correctly focused. When holding your camera vertically, select a horizontal edge for focusing. The split-image circle is for very precise focusing.

If when looking through your viewfinder you see a circle that makes your subject appear clear and then blurred as you turn the focusing ring, you have the microprism focusing aid. With good focusing, your image appears clear and the microprisms stop shimmering. This type of focusing is good for sports and for quick focusing.

The ground-glass viewing screen is generally used in small cameras for focusing close-ups. The image is focused when it appears clear in the viewfinder.

STEPS FOR TAKING PHOTOS

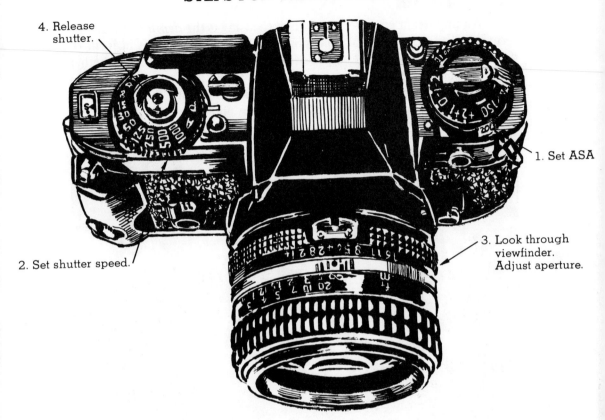

4. Release shutter.

1. Set ASA

2. Set shutter speed.

3. Look through viewfinder. Adjust aperture.

Cameras that have a separate viewing and taking lens have a "brightline" frame with inner "close-up" bracket lines to guide the placement of the subject so that heads are not cut off in the print. This is especially useful when shooting closer than six or seven feet from your subject.

Some simple cameras focus using symbols representing near, medium, and distant shots. Cameras with automatic focusing or with fixed focus need no focusing adjustment.

Here are some suggestions for sharp focusing:

1. *Focus your subject with the lens at its widest opening for brightest viewing.*

2. *Focus on what you select as the center of interest, so that the most important part of your picture will be the sharpest.*

3. *For portrait shots focus on the eye of your subject. A sharp eye makes the whole face seem sharp.*

15

Depth of Field

An important consideration when focusing is the *depth of field*. The term refers to how much of your photo will be in sharp focus in front of and behind your subject. The size of the lens opening determines whether your depth of field will be deep or shallow. Small lens openings, such as f8, f11, and f16, give deep depth of field, with f16 giving the deepest. To photograph a group of people and have them all appear sharply focused, select a small f-stop, an f8 or f11. Focus on a detail one third of the way

Chad Caufield

between the front and the back of the group, and everyone will be recognizable in your photo. Detailed landscapes are usually shot with a small lens opening, with the lens focused on a tree or some other focal point important to your photo. Wide-angle lenses, such as a 28mm, have a built-in deep depth of field. Set at small apertures they are great for candid shots, for they need little or no focusing.

Large lens openings, such as f1.4, f2.8, and f4, put emphasis on your subject by fuzzing up the background. The shallow depth of field works well when the background has distractions and contributes nothing to the subject. Telephoto lenses, such as an 85mm or 135mm, tend to reduce depth of field.

Loading Film in Your Camera

The loading of film in your camera is carefully explained in your camera manual. Be sure to notice whether your rewind knob is turning as you advance the film. If it turns, your film is correctly loaded.

Exposure

Exposure refers to how much light hits the film in the camera to produce an image. Photos that are too dark are caused by the negative not receiving enough light and are called underexposed. Photos that are too light are caused by the negative receiving too much light and are overexposed. What has light got to do with film? Film emulsion contains minute crystals of silver halide. Each tiny grain undergoes a chemical change when light strikes the film. Too much or too little light hitting the film emulsion will produce prints that are too light or too dark; while correct exposure produces an image that has the corresponding light and dark tones of the subject.

The camera balances exposure with three settings: film speed (the ASA or ISO number found on the film box), aperture setting (lens opening), and shutter speed. ASA or ISO numbers refer to the American and International standards rating of a film emulsion's sensitivity to light. This number must be set on the camera for the meter to balance the exposure correctly.

Chad Caufield

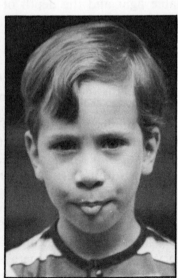

| Underexposed | Normal | Overexposed |

17

F-stops

F-stops indicate the size of the lens opening and are usually found on a ring on the lens barrel. It's important for you to memorize the stops:

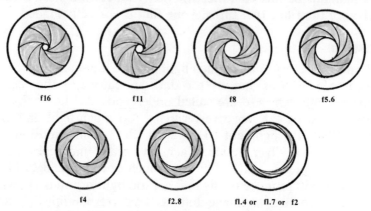

A change from one f-stop to the next smaller lens opening allows only half as much light to enter the camera. For example, stopping down from f4 to f5.6 cuts the amount of light by one half. If you opened up one stop: f4 to f2.8, you would then double the amount of light that would strike the film.

If your camera is aperture-preferred, you first set the f-stop according to the available light and the depth of field desired. The camera's meter will select the appropriate shutter speed to balance the exposure.

Shutters

A camera shutter consists of moving metal or cloth curtains or of overlapping metal leaves that act like a window to the camera's light-tight box. The faster the shutter speed, the less the amount of light that enters the box. Shutter speed numbers are 1000, 500, 250, 125, 60, 30, 15, 8, 4, 2, 1 and *B*. They are generally found on a dial at the top of the camera. These numbers are all fractions of a second: 60 means 1/60, 2 means 1/2, and 1 means 1 full second. As with f-stops, changing from one speed to the next faster shutter speed halves the amount of light for the exposure; and changing to the next slower speed allows twice as much light to enter the lens. The *B* setting is for time exposures. With this setting the lens remains open as long as the shutter release button is depressed. A cable release is a necessary accessory for this. If your camera is shutter-speed preferred, you first select the shutter speed according to the light available and the motion of your subject. Looking through your viewfinder, you will see the f-stop selected by your camera's meter. Freezing fast action, as in sports, requires speeds from 1/500 or faster. For inanimate objects, the shutter speed can be set slower. Slower than 1/60 may require a support or a tripod to hold the camera steady.

Some cameras allow you to select either f-stop or shutter speed. Whichever one you select, the meter selects the other. Cameras that are programmed select both the f-stop and the shutter speed for you. They are programmed for average shooting of average subjects.

To use exposure creatively according to depth of field, available light, and subject motion, remember that f-stops and shutter speeds each work by doubling or halving exposure with each setting change. Whenever you stop the lens down one f-stop (to a smaller opening and less light) from the correct exposure, you need to compensate by changing the shutter speed to the next slower setting (to let in more light). Once your camera's meter balances an exposure, you can select different combinations of f-stops and shutter speeds that will deliver the same amount of light to the film but give more depth of field or more speed. Below is a wedge chart that gives many possible combinations of exposure for *one* suggested light situation; each combination gives exactly the same amount of light for the exposure:

F-STOPS or APERTURES

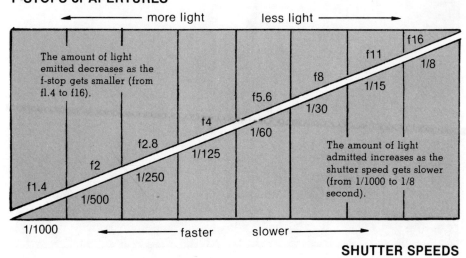

Think of f-stops and shutter speeds as a pair of wedges. Each section of the wedge represents the amount of light sent to the lens in the form of one f-stop. The two wedges together form the exposure. If your meter reads f2.8 at 1/250, you could choose instead f5.6 at 1/60 or any other vertical pair and get the same amount of light for your exposure.

Your camera's meter is designed to take photos of typical scenes on sunny days. It is easily fooled into wrong light readings when light is behind your subject or when your subject is in front of a very dark background. These situations unbalance the meter and result in under- or overexposed prints. To correct the exposure reading under these types of conditions, move in close to your subject. This eliminates the strong light or dark contrasts from your viewfinder. Read the light from the most important part of your subject and then move back to shooting position. Cameras with automatic exposure usually have a way of holding your close-up light reading so that the exposure doesn't change when you step back. If you can't get close to your subject, you can meter the light off the palm of your hand or off a photographer's middle gray card available at photo stores. The middle gray or 18% gray card represents the midpoint between white and black and allows your meter to give balanced readings. The palm of your hand gives the meter similar information. Whichever one you use must be held at the same angle to the light as your subject.

Megan Fuller

When photographing outdoors with a large expanse of sky facing the camera lens, tilt the lens downward so that just a little of the bright sky can be seen in the viewfinder. Determine the exposure, aim the camera to compose your shot, and then shoot.

Photographing skiing, sailing, and beach scenes requires opening up your lens one or two f-stops more than the exposure meter suggests. Many cameras have this +1 and +2 feature. For example, if your camera meters a beach scene at f11 at 1/250, you would change the f-stop to f8 or f5.6 (depending on the brightness) and leave the shutter speed unchanged at 1/250.

At Rock concerts or for spotlighted subjects or events—especially if against a black background—keep the shutter speed that the meter suggests but close down your lens one or two f-stops (for example, change f4 at 1/125 to f8 at 1/125). On automatic-exposure cameras select the −1 or −2 exposure correction.

If your camera meter is totally automatic with no provision for under- or overexposure, you can change the ASA (ISO) setting for a particular shot. Changing ASA 400 to ASA 200 will give you one stop overexposure and lighten your subject by one tone; for two stops overexposure you would change to ASA 100. In reverse, to darken the tone of your subject you could change your film speed's rating of 400, for example, to ASA 800: one stop underexposure. If your film was rated at ASA 100, you could change the setting on your camera to ASA 400 to make your subject two tones darker.

If your batteries fail and your meter stops giving light readings, use this handy guide: in bright sunlight at f16, use the shutter speed closest in number to the ASA of the film you are using. For ASA 100 film, the shutter speed would be 1/125; ASA 400 film would be shot at 1/500. Of course you can shoot at any other combination that gives you the same exposure: remember the wedge!

Sometimes with tricky lighting conditions you may not know whether to keep the meter reading or to change it. In that case, bracket your exposure by taking three shots: one at the meter reading; the second at one f-stop smaller; and the third at one f-stop larger. To bracket an exposure of f8 at 1/125 you would leave the shutter speed at 1/125 and shoot at f8, f5.6, and at f11. One of the exposures will be best for your photo.

Film

Film comes in a variety of speeds numbered by the American Standards Association (ASA) according to its sensitivity to light. High ASA numbers like 400 or 1000 are the most sensitive to light and can be used in dim light without flash. Film for medium bright light would be ASA100 and 125. Brightest light would require ASA32 to 64. When buying film specify the type of camera you will use for the correct size and then select the film according to the light you will shoot with. Specify color daylight film for outdoors and tungsten color film for use with indoor lighting. Buy instant film according to the type of camera you'll use.

Taking Care of Your Camera

To clean lenses give a short huff to moisten and then wipe gently with photo lens cleaning tissue (no other!). A photo blower brush dusts inside and out. Blow before brushing. To prevent major repairs never touch the inside mirror or the curtain that opens and closes the shutter in SLR cameras. Protect from moisture and excessive heat by keeping your camera in a wet proof insulated bag.

The 35mm Single-Lens Reflex System

Although many types of cameras will be used by the readers of this book, much of the information supplied refers to the 35mm single-lens reflex camera, using black-and-white film. I recommend that a serious young photographer use and grow with that system, adding lenses and other accessories, and working in the darkroom with the more economical and challenging film.

3 How to Photograph Your Subject

People

We've come a long way from the earliest portraits when our great grandparents sat vicelike in special seats, holding their poses as the photographer took an unbearably long time to finally shoot the picture. Somehow these Victorian-style portraits all look alike. Today we seldom look for the historic pose; we want personality, character, and naturalness.

To get started photographing people, ask your younger brother or sister or a friend to pose. Have plenty of props handy so it will be fun and your model will not feel self-conscious. Old hats, fun eyeglasses, and making crazy faces help keep up interest and cooperation.

Load the camera and set the ASA if needed. If your camera has point-and-shoot features, you're ready for shooting. If not, preset your f-stop or shutter speed in advance. Read the light off the palm of your hand or set the shutter speed according to the action you expect. This will help you catch your model in motion.

Try different types of shots: some posed and some unposed, or candid. Move to different areas so you can try out different lighting effects—indoors and out.

When the light from a window or from the sky comes from behind your model, open up your lens two f-stops to prevent darkened or underexposed prints. With this type of backlighting, try silhouette effects by closing down your lens two to two-and-one-half f-stops.

David Reif

If you are metering close to your model's face, select an area in shadow, such as under the chin, for black-and-white film. This will give you a richer print, with detail in the shadows. With a flash, have the person look to the left or to the right of the camera to avoid "red eye" or "white eye," depending on the film used.

Position your model so that the sun is not directly in his or her eyes to cause squinting ànd near blindness. Watch for shadows that turn eyes into black sockets and put funny shadows under the nose. Anything that blocks out direct sun rays, such as a building or a wall, will help soften the shadows and put your model in a more cooperative mood.

Consider a few things before you start shooting. How far do you want to be from your model? The farther away you are, the less important your subject becomes. How much background do you want in focus? Control depth of field with the f-stop. How much motion? Select an appropriate shutter speed.

To put your subject at ease, talk about some experience you've had together or something you plan to do together; try a few jokes. No one wants to be directed or ordered about as if a rag doll, so promote sharing and cooperation by asking for suggestions about positions for posing or about what kind of props or activity would be useful. People are more at ease when they're doing something: holding a magazine or a pet. Blowing bubbles, swinging a bat, or bouncing a ball may inspire some good action shots.

Count on 15 to 17 shots before your model begins to forget about the camera. Bring plenty of film and remember that people are more relaxed when they see you know what you are doing.

Nature

If you have a tripod, filters, telephoto and/or wide-angle lenses, bring them along when camping or hiking or just walking in the local park. Look for things in the landscape that you feel are special or different: a tree twisted into a monster shape, a delicate wildflower that would look special with your color film, perhaps a series of rolling hills, one behind the other like phantom ghosts on a foggy day. Whatever attracts your attention and holds your interest should be the subject of your photos.

Eliminate all distractions from your subject by using your depth of field controls with your f-stops; or position yourself so that distracting details are eliminated. Point your camera downward so that the bright sky is mostly eliminated in your viewfinder to avoid underexposed meter readings. Take several shots, changing your position to get a variety of shots to choose from for your final print. Plan to include some type of frame—a branch of a tree or a shrub—to add dimension to your photo.

J. Remick

When using color slide film, underexpose by one-third to one-half f-stop for deeper color saturation.

Watch the horizon line (where land or water meet the sky) in your viewfinder and arrange your composition so it's above or below the exact center. This avoids cutting your picture in half with one section cancelling out the other. A strong composition has one strong element. Horizontal lines, such as a horizon, or verticals, such as trees or posts, should be parallel to the edges of the viewfinder screen unless there is a strong reason for angling them.

Mark O'Neill

Lighting sets the mood for a landscape or nature shot. Early morning and late afternoon light throws long shadows that flow over objects and land to make exciting contour effects. Fields of rippled snow, sand dunes, tilled fields, or long stringy tree roots all reveal abstract patterns when the light is low and the shadows are long. You can eliminate the horizon from your pictures for maximum effectiveness. If you have a telephoto or a wide-angle lens use them. The telephoto lens will compress the view and make things appear closer, while a wide-angle lens will expand the scene and make things appear farther away. Each lens achieves a different expression.

Photographs of waterfalls look convincing when you use a slow shutter speed of 1/8 second to blur the water cascading down the rocks to give a sense of fluid motion. Meter the light on your hand or some object that is a midtone, such as grass or gray rocks. Support your camera on a tripod or against a tree. If you don't have a cable release, let the self-timer trip the shutter for you.

Check your viewfinder top, sides, and bottom for distractions, such as empty bottles, gum wrappers, or windblown newspapers, and remove them if necessary.

At sunset, light changes rapidly. Colors warm and bathe the scene in oranges, fluorescent reds, deep reds, and then purple, as the sun sinks. Meter the light just beside the sun (a gray cloud is helpful for this). If you're using slide film, close down one-third to one-half f-stop for deeper color.

Try some filters that screw into the front of your camera lens. They will darken the sky, cut reflections, and modify tones of black-and-white prints, depending on the filter selected.

Animals

Animals are fun to photograph. You'll need endless patience and an assist from a friend. If you have a lazy cat whose most natural pose is lying about stretched out, start with that. A pet dog that is yappy and constantly jumping up invites some action shots. Animals don't hold poses, so have everything set: film loaded, ASA set, your distance gauged, and your f-stop or shutter speed preset for the action you expect. Large f-stops, such as 1.4 or f2, will fuzz up the background distractions. Move in as close as possible and try some shots at your pet's eye level. Lie flat on the floor or ground with elbows apart for steadiness and shoot at a fraction of a second before the peak of action (your shutter will click at the peak). If you can't get any variety of action, or if your pet is shy and uncooperative, try some jam or honey on the front paws. Or entice your pet with a mechanical toy or a crawling insect. Whistles and strange noises may help with animation. Be kind and coaxing. If using a flash, angle it and, if possible, bounce it off a nearby wall or ceiling. This will prevent the red-eye effect caused by the flash reflecting off the retina in the animal's eye.

Karen Navarro

4 Light

Without light there is no magic. The word photography means "writing with light" and comes from the Greek *phos. Photos*: light, plus *graphos*: writing.

As a photographer you must observe the different types and qualities of light. From sunrise to sunset there is a range of tones, colors, and moods that affect the way photographs look. Shadows lengthen and contract and hard edges turn into soft outlines depending on the positions of the sun. At dawn the colors are muted; by early afternoon they are full and strong. The golden light of late afternoon becomes cooler and then more mysterious at twilight.

The direction of the light hitting your subject is important:

a. Side lighting gives dimension and strong texture and pattern to your pictures indoors and out.
b. Back lighting darkens foreground subjects. Dramatic silhouette effects are possible by underexposing one and one-half to two f-stops more than your light meter indicates. To lighten a back-lighted subject, overexpose one and one-half to two f-stops.
c. Front lighting, inside and outside, flattens out form and textures.

Weather is a light designer. Cloudy bright days give soft, diffused, even light. Foggy overcast rainy days create mood for picture taking: loneliness, isolation, even mystery. To shoot in rainy weather, enclose your camera in a large plastic bag and just allow the lens— equipped with a skylight filter—to emerge from the opening (a rubber band around the lens barrel will hold the bag snug). Also, don't forget an umbrella and lens tissue.

Bright sunlight, though perfect for photos, can have its drawbacks: highlights can bleach out and shadows can become like black holes.What can you do about this? Try moving your subject where there is mostly shade or diffused light. This will cut down the extreme contrasts in tone that your film may not be able to register. Also, blocking out direct sun with a building or some object helps diffuse the light.

Winter light can reveal tree branches, shrubs, and fields sculpted into new shapes by snow. Look for the vivid color of ski clothes against winter white; the action of people ice skating or skiing; ski-track patterns or patterns created by the wind in the snow; light shining on icy branches with diamond radiance. Have your camera handy, and as you discover these wonders record them in your own special way. To shoot, open up your lens one to two f-stops to avoid underexposed prints.

Indoor Shooting

For indoor shooting using available light, without flash, use a fast film: ASA (ISO) 400. Wide lens openings, such as f2.8 or f1.7, will eliminate distracting details. Getting close to your subject will help fill the frame without unnecessary background.

When interior detail is important to your photo, arrange the room lighting so that it is bright enough and coming from a desirable direction to help you close down the lens to f8. For color film with tungsten light, be sure to use tungsten film for correct color balance. Daylight color film will give a warm tone when there is an equal balance of natural and tungsten light. Indoors as well as outdoors you can use flash as a "fill" light to avoid undesirable dark features. Try using a single layer of a white handkerchief over the flash to soften the light. This prevents it from washing out the features or causing "red" eye. If using flash, remember to set the shutter speed for the sync setting for your camera (usually 1/60 or sometimes 1/125; check your camera manual for this).

Outdoor Shooting

In cities, light in the late afternoon is especially dramatic. Look for long shadows that create strong and unexpected patterns on old buildings, cobbled streets, and sculpture surfaces.

Sunsets are always challenging. Try shooting just before the sun hits the horizon or when it's partially hidden behind a branch or building for a radiant effect. Meter just beside the sun (a gray cloud is good) and open up one to two f-stops to avoid underexposing your film.

When shooting with color at dusk, the glow of light against a dark blue sky will give the impression of nighttime. As the light grows dimmer —a good time is an hour after sunset—try for pattern shots of neon and dazzling color with time exposures in the big cities or at the lighted rides at fairs or amusement parks. Focus on the lights and stop the lens down to f16. Leave the shutter open for 2 to 4 seconds. Use 400 ASA film, a tripod to support your camera, and a cable release to release the shutter, and set your shutter speed on *B*.

For fireworks use fast film and set the camera lens at f11 or f16. Open your shutter for the first burst of explosions, then, keeping the shutter open, cover the lens with a piece of opaque cardboard until the second burst. Repeat again with the cardboard and release the shutter after two or three bursts. A telephoto lens helps bring the whole display closer. What could you do with a zoom lens?

Other nighttime subjects for dramatic effects are floodlit buildings and monuments, brightly lit streets, and panoramic views for city traffic patterns taken from observation decks or high buildings. These require time exposures with the shutter set at *B*. Bracket your shots until you have gotten some experience and have developed a sense of how light can work for you at night.

Jeff Fitter

Gary Gastman

5 Composing the Picture

How can you get your photos to be dynamic and to say something important; to look different from most of the pictures that come back from the drugstore or photomat?

People can like your photos because of the subject matter: babies, puppies, and kittens always make a hit. But to get beyond the subject matter and really produce an *important* photo requires something called *composition*.

Here are some suggestions to get you started:

1. Subject. Identify what your subject is when looking through the viewfinder. A person or a group can be your subject; but so can a mood, an expression, or an awe-inspiring scene, such as a moonscape or setting sun. Select only one subject for your photo. Two rival shapes in your viewfinder are better separated into two photos. Or, if you prefer, increase the size of one (have it closer to the camera lens) or crop the rival shape so that it loses importance.
2. Contrast. Allow your selected subject to emerge by being a different tone from its background. With too little tonal contrast the eye loses interest.

Jean Fitzpatrick

Robert A. Kern

3. Focal Point. Decide on a focal point for your subject. If it's a portrait of your Aunt Sally, it might be the eyes or the hands. Decide on the particular area you want to draw attention to. Lines can help with this. Just as the lines of train tracks lead into the distance by the way they converge to a point, so paths, streams, roads, fences, shadows, and even folds of clothing or blankets can lead the eye to your main point of interest.

4. Mood. Lines can also help create mood. Horizontal lines may create a sense of peace and calm. Vertical lines may give a sense of excitement, power, dignity, and majesty, as in photos of tall trees in the forest.

5. Placement. Where do you place the subject? Some photographers use a device called "thirds" to place important lines or subjects. As you look through your viewfinder, imagine it is a rec-

Wayne Johnson

Megan Fuller

tangle divided horizontally and vertically into thirds. The lines and the places where they intersect are guides for placing important shapes. (Notice that the "thirds" system automatically eliminates placing things dead center, including horizon lines, poles, and trees.)

6. **Angle of view.** The way you point your camera can add to the expressive power of your composition. With your camera pointing up at your subject, you create photos that are expressions of power or aggressiveness. Pointing your camera down at your subject can give the photo's subject the impression of smallness, weakness, perhaps something fragile.

7. **Diagonal lines.** To suggest energy or action diagonal lines are helpful. When they go from corner to corner of your viewfinder, they can weaken your composition by dividing your photo into two equal static parts.

In general, consider a photo balanced when the eye travels to all of the elements you've selected to show. Contrast helps with balancing, for it can help lead the eye around the composition. A small white accent in a large silhouetted or darkened shape will attract attention. Also, white shapes appear larger when surrounded by dark areas than do dark shapes on white or light areas. Visually, white may carry more weight than black and need more black to balance it.

With color film, vivid contrasting colors act to draw the eye to the focal point and can add balance to your photo. Contrast brings emphasis to your subject. A medium-gray subject against a medium-gray background produces a throw-away photo. Place the subject on a dark or lighter toned background and the subject is important again because it can be seen. Arrange your shooting angle to eliminate distracting clutter, or if possible bury it in a sea of similar tones. Emphasis by contrast can also be made by using patterns or textures that contrast with the subject. Size is also helpful for emphasis. To show how tall a star basketball player is contrast the player with someone who is short. This is true for showing fatness against thin, and large against small.

Jordi Visser

Tom Hemrick

The blur of motion can contrast with static backgrounds and emphasize your subject. Subjects in motion require more space—for potential motion—in the direction in which the motion is headed. This is true also for your subject's eyes that may be looking up or down or to the side. They need room to look into.

Another way to get emphasis is to show the unexpected. If all of the marchers in a parade are in step except one, you can guess who will get the attention. These are just some of the ways to focus attention on your subject. You will discover other ways as you gain experience producing photos.

Marchers in a parade form patterns and rhythms with their bodies, arms, and legs. The pattern itself or the rhythm can be the subject of your photo.

Rolling hills and any repetition of similar basic shapes can create visually exciting photographs. Shadows can be a source of abstract rhythmic patterns. Whenever possible try to avoid breaking up the pattern with a horizon line unless the line adds a special dimension to your composition.

Look for simple formations, such as triangles, rectangles, or diamond shapes, to organize and strengthen your photo. Three people in a group—one standing in the center and two kneeling on either side—form a triangular arrangement, as do four singular trees in a woods spaced to form a rectangle or a diamond shape. Arrangements like these help to concentrate attention on your subject.

Experience, practice, and awareness will help you develop your "camera eye." You will no longer be taking pictures; you'll be making them.

Finding a Personal Vision

A good way to develop your kind of photography—your own visual language—is to work with subjects you are familiar with. Walk down some of the streets of your city or town. If you are civic-minded, what do you see that needs improvement? Streets cluttered with debris? Take some pictures of this and present them to the town or city council. If your photos provide strong evidence, they may listen and act. Streets jammed due to lack of parking space? Get your camera into action and prove a point. Submit some of your revealing photographs to the local newspapers, and you'll be on your way to becoming a photo journalist. School newspapers will be eager to publish your photos and will help you in your interest to make things better.

Let your photos show people (and yourself) that your town has good things—things that they might have forgotten or may have not seen in the way your photos show. Try a photo essay on this.

Other ways to put your camera to work for you might include using it in your schoolwork to illustrate information you present in themes or essays; compiling an original family album for a gift (perhaps a record spanning one year); and/or taking photos of stores, factories, or offices for local citizens. Entering contests will also help you gain experience and give you incentive to produce better photographs.

After you've accumulated quite a number of photos, line up a batch of them to see where your interests lie: with people, animals, architecture, or nature. See what caught your eye. Was it special lighting effects, patterns and details of nature, people and their expressions, or abstract shapes and textures? What kind of viewpoint seems to be surfacing most often? Let that be an area for further picture taking. Be ready always to take a fresh new direction when your interest shifts.

Start a collection of your photos: it could be a scrapbook or a portfolio. This will keep your work organized and ready to be shown when you desire.

You are your camera. For it is you who will find and record the shape of a tree, an expression on a face, or bring out the visual sense of a mood—whether it be loneliness, sadness, excitement, or joy.

6 The Darkroom

Shooting photographs of your favorite subjects is only a part of photography's creative potential. Developing film to produce negatives for printing and then the "magic show" of recreating your shots on a blank white sheet of printing paper opens the door to a lifetime interest that grows more challenging as you learn and work at it.

Reeling the Film

To produce prints of your photos you have to develop your negatives. This is easily done by using a photographer's changing bag: a portable darkroom that prevents light from hitting the film. In the bag the film is wound onto a reel that allows every part of the film to be exposed to the chemicals needed to produce workable negatives. When loaded, the reel is placed in its light-tight tank and covered with a top that contains a cap. The tank is then removed from the changing bag, and all processing with chemicals can be done in daylight. The top cap is removed—the tank is still light-proof—so that the chemicals can be poured into the center hole.

Here are the steps in processing negatives of black-and-white film:

1. Film developer: time required for development is found on the information sheet that comes with the film.

2. Water: to stop the developer's action.

3. Fixer: to fix the image and make it permanent. After fixing, the cover can be taken off the tank and the film exposed to light.

4. Running water bath: to wash away the fixer or hypo.

5. Hyponeutralizer: to neutralize any remaining fixer.

6. Running water bath: to wash away any remaining fixer.

7. Wetting agent: to prevent water marks on the film.

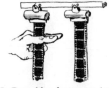

8. Run film between two of your fingers to remove moisture. Hang with clothespins to dry in a dust-free place.

All processing is done with chemicals that should be about 68 °F. Directions for agitating the film in the chemicals are supplied with the developing tank.

Protecting and Filing Negatives

When the negatives are completely dry, lay them on a clean surface to cut into strips. Count all the frames before cutting, and plan your cuts so that you will have five frames per strip, even if you have to use the black ends to make a full strip. A negative file will store all the exposures you shot from one cartridge and can be marked with dates and subject and neatly stored in a three-ring hard-cover binder. Vinyl or glassine negative sleeves, available at photo shops, can be used for storing individual strips.

Printing in the Darkroom

Once you get involved with photography, you'll want to do your own printing and enlarging. You might plan for a dry darkroom in your bedroom, a section of your basement, or even a closet or a corner of the garage. Bathrooms and laundry rooms are good places, for they have running water. But running water is not necessary. Photographers joke about creating darkrooms by closing their eyes.

Here are some basic needs for the darkroom dry area:

1. *Light-proof room or area.*
2. *Place to store chemicals; shelves are helpful.*
3. *Countertop for an enlarger and printing paper.*
4. *Worktable or counter large enough to hold trays for the chemicals.*

Darkrooms are best planned with separate wet (chemical trays) and dry (enlarger work) areas. Some basic accessories for the darkroom:

DRY AREA

1. Enlarger with lens and a negative carrier for your film (with most cameras you will use 35mm film).

2. Safelight with filter: OC filters are used for most black-and-white papers.

3. Focusing aid: a grain magnifier or focuser.

4. Blower brush to remove dust from negatives.

5. Timer for enlarger.

6. Dodging and burning-in tools.

7. Enlarging easel.

8. Blotter book for drying prints.

9. Sheet of 8" x 10" plate glass to hold negatives flat on the easel when making contact prints.

10. 8" x 10" piece of cardboard.

11. Some type of ventilation.

WET AREA

12. Four (4) plastic photo trays to hold paper developer, stop, fixer, and hyponeutralizer.

13. Timer — can be a kitchen timer for timing chemical actions.

14. Four (4) bamboo tongs — one for each tray.

15. Funnel.

16. Dish basin to hold wet processed prints.

17. Gooseneck lamp with 15-watt bulb to be mounted or placed near developer tray.

18. Roll of paper towels.

19. Chemicals mixed according to directions.

20. Clean soft sponge to wipe water off the print surface.

A "contact" sheet is usually the first print made from negatives. It shows all your shots on one 8″ × 10″ sheet. Using a magnifying glass, you can select and mark the negatives you wish to enlarge. To make the contact sheet, make a sandwich of printing paper, negatives in the negative file, and glass to hold the negatives flat. The sandwich is exposed to the light of the enlarger and then processed in the printing chemicals. All actual printing is done under safelight.

Test strip

Nancy Mistretta

1. Negative is placed in enlarger.

2. Beam light through negative onto light-sensitive paper.

3. Developer brings out the positive image on your printing paper.

4. An acid bath stops the developer action.

5. Fixer washes away undeveloped particles of silver.

6. Hyponeutralizer neutralizes fixer.

7. Final water rinse clears away all chemicals.

8. The final print.

Making an enlargement: When the white sheet of printing paper gradually and magically becomes a recognizable image as it is rocked in the developer, it produces a sense of reward and wonder as well.

The enlargement, or print, involves centering a negative in the enlarger's negative carrier and focusing the light and the image on focusing paper that has been put in an easel. A grain focuser helps with sharp focus. Prints are usually made with the enlarger lens set at f8 or f11. To find the best time for exposure, a test strip is used. This is a small piece cut from your printing paper and placed over an important part of the image projected on the easel. The timer is set for three seconds and with the help of a piece of cardboard the strip is given successive three-second exposures. The darkest tone on the test strip has the most time, and the lightest has the least.

Look at the test strip in regular room light to select the best exposure. Set the timer for that time, and under safelight only, place your printing paper in the easel and expose it to the enlarger light. The print is now removed from the easel, ready for its chemical bath. It is placed in the paper developer and gently rocked in the tray for about two to three minutes while the image emerges. It is drained and placed into the stop bath. Again it is drained—to avoid chemical contamination—and goes from there to the fixer and then drained carefully and placed into the hyponeutralizer.

All the chemicals require slow, steady rocking of the trays. If your darkroom is dry, your print will go into a water holding bath until you are ready to wash it in running water for the time required by the paper you use. A damp sponge removes surface moisture. Your prints can be dried in a photo blotter book and later pressed under some heavy weights.

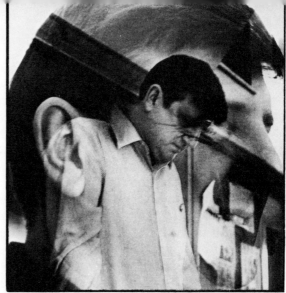

Chad Caufield

7 Some Experiments that Add Excitement

As you become more practiced and more satisfied with your photographs, you may wish to try some print manipulations and experiments. Here are a few to get you started.

For the Camera

Double Exposures: Deliberately planned, double-exposure shooting can produce exciting results. You can achieve all kinds of rare, odd, distorted, funny, and mysterious pictures by incorporating people, animals, and other elements in the most unexpected places and situations.

Double-exposure shooting means exposing your unit of film twice or more for one photograph. Many of the current cameras provide for double exposure, but some don't. In either case, consult your camera's manual. If no instructions are given, try this: push the rewind button (usually at the bottom of your camera). Turn the rewind crank, in the direction of the arrow, to rotate a full 360°. Wind the shutter for the second exposure *while holding the rewind crank to prevent slipping.* You can shoot two or more exposures. A different f-stop or shutter speed may be used for your second (or third) exposure. The additional exposure could be a close-up of a detail or—by backing away—a smaller image. Try to visualize what you want the multiple images to look like and how one will fit with another on the same frame.

Another multiple-exposure experiment uses an opaque mask to cover half the camera lens (an old lens cap with half cut out works well). The cap or mask is adjusted so that when you look in the viewfinder you see only half the viewing screen. Mark the position of the cap or mask with white pencil or a tiny edge of tape on the lens barrel. Make the first exposure, then rotate the cap or move the mask so that it covers that part of the viewfinder that was left open for the first exposure. Now make the second exposure. The whole film frame is now covered by the two separate exposures. This is the way to have the same person appear twice in one picture. Using the camera's self-timer and a tripod, that person could be you. To work well, be sure the half-mask fits close to the lens, or the joining of the two halves will not mesh. There are filters available that make this easy to do.

Motion: Experiment with motion by using a slow shutter speed to produce a streak of motion. Another way to show motion is by keeping the moving subject in good focus but streaking the background. This requires a technique called *panning*. You simply set your shutter speed for 1/30 or slower and while looking through the viewfinder move just your camera so the lens follows the action. This effect gives more sense of motion than just freezing an action.

Remember that action is fastest when viewed at a 90° angle and slows as you or your subject move forward or backward to create a shallower angle. The slowest apparent speed is action coming directly toward you or going directly away from you.

Playing With Reflections: Reflections can lead to different and unexpected ways to view a subject. They are more interesting when there is some kind of planned distortion. To stimulate your imagination, here are some possibilities for photos. After a rain, look for puddles reflecting people, buildings, or traffic; look especially for puddles rippled by a breeze. Glass or mirrored walls of giant office buildings that throw reflections of each other back and forth, or perhaps of much older buildings, give a sense of time and space. Search the glass of store windows for exciting and unexpected reflections.

Mirrors, and mirrors reflecting your subject, can help create special moods—thoughtful, playful, even tricky. Mirrorlike surfaces such as aluminum foil or mirrored mylar can be curved or shaped in many ways to create unlimited distortion. Your subject could be a strong pattern—one as simple as bold black-and-white stripes. Bubbles, shiny metal parts of cars, bikes, musical instruments, as well as lakes or reflecting pools are all worthy of investigation. The way you see and interpret the mirrored images in your photos—the way you select just the right view—will reveal and share with others your personal vision.

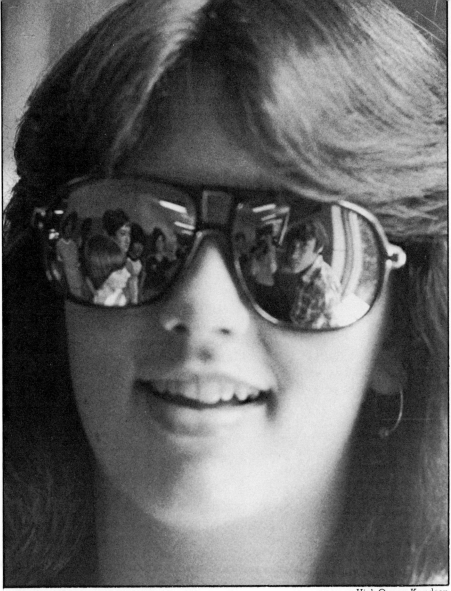

For the Darkroom

Two basic types of print manipulation used to improve prints can also be used in creative experimental ways. *Dodging* allows less light to hit an area so that it will be lighter in tone. Either your hands or dodging tools are used for this, depending on the size and shape of the area you want to lighten. Dodging tools are simply small opaque shapes—usually circles, ovals, triangles, and so on—that fit into a thin wire about eight inches long with a coil at one end to slip the shapes into. They can be purchased in a photo store or can be made easily.

Dodging tool for holding back light for part of exposure time.

Burning-in tool (cardboard with hole) adds to exposure time.

The closer the opaque shape is held to the enlarger lens, the larger the shadow it throws on the enlarging paper. If the dodger is held closer to the printing paper, the shadow will be smaller. The cast shadow blocks the enlarger light and prevents that area from printing dark. Whether you use your hands or the dodging tool, they must be in constant back-and-forth and up-and-down motion within the desired area so that the projected shadow becomes blurred and blends into the rest of the print. Dodging is done during the first exposure. Using this manipulation, you can see how whole areas of the print can be held back and how a second negative could be projected into that area for a multiple exposure.

The opposite of dodging is *burning-in*, which darkens selected areas of your print. Unlike dodging, burning-in is done after the first exposure. Parts to be darkened are exposed again for full and sometimes a third exposure. Your hands can be used to shield part of the print while you expose the rest. A good way to start is by using a cardboard a bit larger than your print that has a hole in the center. The hole should be smaller than the part of your print you wish to darken but large enough to do the job.

Again, the closer you hold the cardboard to the enlarger lens, the larger the hole will appear and the more light will be let in for increased exposure. The closer the cardboard is to the paper in the easel, the smaller the exposed area. The image will be projected on the cardboard as it is held under the enlarger during exposure. The projection will help you locate the area you want to make darker. To avoid circles on your print, move the cardboard back and forth and up and down to blur the outline.

To burn in a sky or a corner or edge of a print, an uncut cardboard a bit larger than your print can shield all sections of the print while the rest gets additional exposure. Slowly pass the cardboard back and forth, covering and then uncovering the area to be darkened for the required length of time. Burning-in helps tone down areas that might attract attention from the main subject of your print. It can also create some eerie and mysterious effects.

R. Fusco

8 Where to Learn More

With your first camera you'll begin to experience the joy and excitement that has kept millions of people around the world clicking their shutters. Your photos will express a universal language to which everyone can respond.

Perhaps you will make photography a serious hobby, or it may become your life's work.

There are many sources available that can help you grow as a photographer. Join a nearby camera club, where you can share information, outings, companionship, and competition with other photography buffs. Meetings are generally held twice a month, and dues are low, considering what they offer.

Check out the available photo magazines at the library. Among the most popular are:

Petersen's Photographic
P.O. Box 3414
Los Angeles, CA 90028

Popular Photography
Ziff-Davis Publishing Co.
One Park Ave.
New York, NY 10016

Camera 35
Popular Publications, Inc.
420 Lexington Ave.
New York, NY 10017

Modern Photography
130 E. 59th St.
New York, NY 10022

Darkroom Techniques
P.O. Box 48312
6366 Gross Point Rd.
Niles, IL 60648

The Photo
P.O. Box MC
32275 Mally Road
Madison Hts., MI

45

Libraries will usually order any photography books you request that they do not have. Some helpful books are listed below:

Life Library of Photography
Time-Life Books
New York, NY 10020.
Seventeen volumes, each containing information on an important aspect of photography.

SLR Photographers Handbook
Carl Shipman
H.P. Books
P.O. Box 5367
Tucson, AZ 85703.

John Hedgecoe's Complete Photography Course
Simon & Schuster
New York, NY
A step-by-step guide to picture making, with over 700 illustrations, many in color.

The Darkroom Handbook,
by D. Curtin & J. DeMaio Van Nostrand Reinhold Co., NY. A complete guide to designing, constructing, and equipping a darkroom, whether it be a closet or a bathroom makeshift photo lab or a custom professional job.

Watson-Guptill Publishers will send you a list of their **Amphoto** *books. Write them at:* P.O. Box 2014, Lakewood, NJ 08701.

The Kodak Company is an unlimited resource for information, books, and pamphlets. Write for their **Index to Kodak Information L-5,** Eastman Kodak Co., Rochester, NY 14650.

If you have any questions concerning any aspect of photography, write them c/o Photo Information Dept. 841, Rochester, NY 14650.

The editors of the Kodak Company have recently produced two good hardcover books on photography: **Joy of Photography** *and* **More Joy of Photography.** *They are published by the Addison Wesley Publishing Co., Reading, MA.*

For experimenting and trying new things with photography look for the following books:

100 Camera Projects for Fun and Profit,
by John Durniak Ziff-Davis Publishing Co. One Park Ave. New York, NY 10016.

Design by Photography *and* **Creative Photography,** *by Otto Croy Visual Communications Books Hastings House Publishers 10 E. 40th St. New York, NY 10016.*

Another great resource is the **National Geographic magazine,** *published by the National Geographic Society Washington, D.C., Study the magnificent photography in magazines. Seeing good photos can be an aid to producing good photos.*

If there are photography galleries available or some special photography exhibits, plan to visit them. Attempt to understand what makes the photographs worthy of public showing.

As a young photographer, you will be concerned at first mostly with the mechanics of photography. By constantly looking, making every unique sight a potential photo, and by striving to improve your photos, to strengthen the design, to catch and emphasize the special expression or effect, and by working with light and exposure to make them expressive, you will begin to develop that "third eye" that shifts your work from technology to personal vision—from the mundane to the poetic. There's a big world out there, and your camera is waiting to explore it with you!

Glossary of Terms

Aperture: an adjustable or fixed opening in a camera through which light enters to reach the film. Aperture size is calibrated in f-numbers or -stops; the larger the f-stop number, the smaller the lens opening to admit light.

ASA: American Standards Association devised a system along with ISO (International Standards Organization) for rating the speed or light sensitivity of film emulsions.

Automatic Camera: a camera with a built-in exposure meter that can automatically adjust the shutter or the lens opening or both for exposure.

Back lighting: light coming from behind the subject; can produce silhouette effects.

B (bulb) setting: a shutter-speed setting on an adjustable camera that allows for time exposures; the shutter stays open as long as the release button is held down.

Cable release: a length of flexible cable that allows a camera shutter to open by pressing a plunger on the end. The other end screws into the shutter release button.

Cassette: container for 35mm film. After exposure, the film is rewound onto the spool of the cassette before the camera is opened.

Color negative film: film that gives color negatives for prints.

Color reversal film: film that gives color positives—slides or transparencies.

Contact sheet: a print made by exposing light sensitive paper in contact with negatives. It is used to help select those negatives which are to be enlarged.

Density: the opaqueness of a negative or the blackness of a print.

Depth of field: the distance range between the nearest and farthest objects from the camera that appear in sharp focus in a print. Smallest lens openings produce the greatest depth of field—f8, f11, f16, and so on.

Dodging: a technique used in printing photos where one area of a print gets less exposure than the rest.

Emulsion: the light-sensitive layer of a photographic material. It consists essentially of silver halide crystals suspended in gelatin.

Enlargement: a print made larger than the original image on the film.

Exposure: the amount of light allowed to reach the light-sensitive material during formation of the latent image. Exposure depends on the brightness of the image, the aperture setting, and the shutter-speed setting, plus the emulsion speed of the film or paper used.

Filter: a small gelatin or glass used to block a specific part of the light passing through it or to change or distort the image in some way.

Flash synchronization (sync): coordination of both flash unit and camera so that the flash fires when the shutter is open.

Gray card: a neutral gray-colored cardboard that reflects 18 percent of the light falling on it.

Guide number: indicates the effective power of a flash unit. For a given film speed, the guide number divided by the distance between the flash and the subject gives the correct f-stop to use.

Hot shoe: built into many cameras to provide a live contact for firing a flash unit.

Incident light: light falling on the subject. Some light meters read only incident light instead of reflective light (light reflected off a subject). Some light meters read both types of light.

Negative: an image on transparent film that records light tones as dark and vice versa; in color negatives every color is represented by the complementary color of the original subject.

Normal lens: a lens that produces an image closest to the perspective that the eye sees.

Panchromatic: a type of emulsion used for most black-and-white film. It is sensitive to all visible colors.

Panning: moving a camera to photograph a moving subject while keeping the image of the subject in the same relative position in the viewfinder.

Photogram: print formed by placing objects on light sensitive paper, exposed to light for a few seconds and then developed.

Positive: opposite of a negative. The tones of the image are the same tones as the original subject.

Reflex camera: a camera that uses mirrors or prisms to reflect an image onto a screen for focusing and composition.

Resin-coated paper: photo-printing paper with a synthetic resin coating to prevent excessive absorption of liquids during processing. It can be washed and dried more quickly than untreated paper, but limits some types of photo processing.

Safelight: a special darkroom lamp of a color that will not affect photo materials being used.

Shutter: blades, curtain, a plate, or some other moveable plane in a camera that controls the time of the exposure of light to the film.

Solarization: exposing a print to a short burst of dim light while it is still in the developer.

Stopping down: changing the lens opening from larger to smaller—f8 to f11, and so on.

Test strip: a strip of light sensitive paper exposed to increasing intervals of light to determine which of the exposures is most suitable for the print to be made.

Tungsten: a common source of indoor light.

Zoom lens: a lens whose focusing remains unchanged while its focal length can be adjusted over a wide range.

INDEX